DINE ON A DIME!

Meal Planner and Budget Organizer

@ Journals & Notebooks

Copyright 2016

All Rights reserved. No part of this book may be reproduced or used in any way or formor by any means whether electronic or mechanical, this means that you cannot recordor photocopy any material ideas or tips that are provided in this book.

	MONDAY	TUESDAY	WEDNESDAY	THURSDAY
Breakfast				
Lunch				
Dinner				

	FRIDAY	SATURDAY	SUNDAY	NOTES
Breakfast				
Lunch				
Dinner				

Budget Planner

Expense	Amount	Due Date
UTILITIES		
Electric		
Gas		
Electric		
Electric		
Electric		
TRANSPORTATION		
Car Payment		
Gas		
Repair / Maintenance		
DEBT PAYMENTS		
Credit Card		
Others		
MISC.		
Groceries		
Personal Care		
Household items		
TOTAL		

	MONDAY	TUESDAY	WEDNESDAY	THURSDAY
Breakfast				
Lunch				
Dinner				

	FRIDAY	SATURDAY	SUNDAY	NOTES
Breakfast				
Lunch				
Dinner				

Budget Planner

Expense	Amount	Due Date
UTILITIES		
Electric		
Gas		
Electric		
Electric		
Electric		
TRANSPORTATION		
Car Payment		
Gas		
Repair / Maintenance		
DEBT PAYMENTS		
Credit Card		
Others		
MISC.		
Groceries		
Personal Care		
Household items		
TOTAL		

	MONDAY	TUESDAY	WEDNESDAY	THURSDAY
Breakfast				
Lunch				
Dinner				

	FRIDAY	SATURDAY	SUNDAY	NOTES
Breakfast				
Lunch				
Dinner				

Budget Planner

Expense	Amount	Due Date
UTILITIES		
Electric		
Gas		
Electric		
Electric		
Electric		
TRANSPORTATION		
Car Payment		
Gas		
Repair / Maintenance		
DEBT PAYMENTS		
Credit Card		
Others		
MISC.		
Groceries		
Personal Care		
Household items		
TOTAL		

	MONDAY	TUESDAY	WEDNESDAY	THURSDAY
Breakfast				
Lunch				
Dinner				

	FRIDAY	SATURDAY	SUNDAY	NOTES
Breakfast				
Lunch				
Dinner				

Budget Planner

Expense	Amount	Due Date
UTILITIES		
Electric		
Gas		
Electric		
Electric		
Electric		
TRANSPORTATION		
Car Payment		
Gas		
Repair / Maintenance		
DEBT PAYMENTS		
Credit Card		
Others		
MISC.		
Groceries		
Personal Care		
Household items		
TOTAL		

	MONDAY	TUESDAY	WEDNESDAY	THURSDAY
Breakfast				
Lunch				
Dinner				

	FRIDAY	SATURDAY	SUNDAY	NOTES
Breakfast				
Lunch				
Dinner				

Budget Planner

Expense	Amount	Due Date
UTILITIES		
Electric		
Gas		
Electric		
Electric		
Electric		
TRANSPORTATION		
Car Payment		
Gas		
Repair / Maintenance		
DEBT PAYMENTS		
Credit Card		
Others		
MISC.		
Groceries		
Personal Care		
Household items		
TOTAL		

	MONDAY	TUESDAY	WEDNESDAY	THURSDAY
Breakfast				
Lunch				
Dinner				

	FRIDAY	SATURDAY	SUNDAY	NOTES
Breakfast				
Lunch				
Dinner				

Budget Planner

Expense	Amount	Due Date
UTILITIES		
Electric		
Gas		
Electric		
Electric		
Electric		
TRANSPORTATION		
Car Payment		
Gas		
Repair / Maintenance		
DEBT PAYMENTS		
Credit Card		
Others		
MISC.		
Groceries		
Personal Care		
Household items		
TOTAL		

	MONDAY	TUESDAY	WEDNESDAY	THURSDAY
Breakfast				
Lunch				
Dinner				

	FRIDAY	SATURDAY	SUNDAY	NOTES
Breakfast				
Lunch				
Dinner				

Budget Planner

Expense	Amount	Due Date
UTILITIES		
Electric		
Gas		
Electric		
Electric		
Electric		
TRANSPORTATION		
Car Payment		
Gas		
Repair / Maintenance		
DEBT PAYMENTS		
Credit Card		
Others		
MISC.		
Groceries		
Personal Care		
Household items		
TOTAL		

	MONDAY	TUESDAY	WEDNESDAY	THURSDAY
Breakfast				
Lunch				
Dinner				

	FRIDAY	SATURDAY	SUNDAY	NOTES
Breakfast				
Lunch				
Dinner				

Budget Planner

Expense	Amount	Due Date
UTILITIES		
Electric		
Gas		
Electric		
Electric		
Electric		
TRANSPORTATION		
Car Payment		
Gas		
Repair / Maintenance		
DEBT PAYMENTS		
Credit Card		
Others		
MISC.		
Groceries		
Personal Care		
Household items		
TOTAL		

	MONDAY	TUESDAY	WEDNESDAY	THURSDAY
Breakfast				
Lunch				
Dinner				

	FRIDAY	SATURDAY	SUNDAY	NOTES
Breakfast				
Lunch				
Dinner				

Budget Planner

Expense	Amount	Due Date
UTILITIES		
Electric		
Gas		
Electric		
Electric		
Electric		
TRANSPORTATION		
Car Payment		
Gas		
Repair / Maintenance		
DEBT PAYMENTS		
Credit Card		
Others		
MISC.		
Groceries		
Personal Care		
Household items		
TOTAL		

	MONDAY	TUESDAY	WEDNESDAY	THURSDAY
Breakfast				
Lunch				
Dinner				

	FRIDAY	SATURDAY	SUNDAY	NOTES
Breakfast				
Lunch				
Dinner				

Budget Planner

Expense	Amount	Due Date
UTILITIES		
Electric		
Gas		
Electric		
Electric		
Electric		
TRANSPORTATION		
Car Payment		
Gas		
Repair / Maintenance		
DEBT PAYMENTS		
Credit Card		
Others		
MISC.		
Groceries		
Personal Care		
Household items		
TOTAL		

	MONDAY	TUESDAY	WEDNESDAY	THURSDAY
Breakfast				
Lunch				
Dinner				

	FRIDAY	SATURDAY	SUNDAY	NOTES
Breakfast				
Lunch				
Dinner				

Budget Planner

Expense	Amount	Due Date
UTILITIES		
Electric		
Gas		
Electric		
Electric		
Electric		
TRANSPORTATION		
Car Payment		
Gas		
Repair / Maintenance		
DEBT PAYMENTS		
Credit Card		
Others		
MISC.		
Groceries		
Personal Care		
Household items		
TOTAL		

	MONDAY	TUESDAY	WEDNESDAY	THURSDAY
Breakfast				
Lunch				
Dinner				

	FRIDAY	SATURDAY	SUNDAY	NOTES
Breakfast				
Lunch				
Dinner				

Budget Planner

Expense	Amount	Due Date
UTILITIES		
Electric		
Gas		
Electric		
Electric		
Electric		
TRANSPORTATION		
Car Payment		
Gas		
Repair / Maintenance		
DEBT PAYMENTS		
Credit Card		
Others		
MISC.		
Groceries		
Personal Care		
Household items		
TOTAL		

	MONDAY	TUESDAY	WEDNESDAY	THURSDAY
Breakfast				
Lunch				
Dinner				

	FRIDAY	SATURDAY	SUNDAY	NOTES
Breakfast				
Lunch				
Dinner				

Budget Planner

Expense	Amount	Due Date
UTILITIES		
Electric		
Gas		
Electric		
Electric		
Electric		
TRANSPORTATION		
Car Payment		
Gas		
Repair / Maintenance		
DEBT PAYMENTS		
Credit Card		
Others		
MISC.		
Groceries		
Personal Care		
Household items		
TOTAL		

	MONDAY	TUESDAY	WEDNESDAY	THURSDAY
Breakfast				
Lunch				
Dinner				

	FRIDAY	SATURDAY	SUNDAY	NOTES
Breakfast				
Lunch				
Dinner				

Budget Planner

Expense	Amount	Due Date
UTILITIES		
Electric		
Gas		
Electric		
Electric		
Electric		
TRANSPORTATION		
Car Payment		
Gas		
Repair / Maintenance		
DEBT PAYMENTS		
Credit Card		
Others		
MISC.		
Groceries		
Personal Care		
Household items		
TOTAL		

	MONDAY	TUESDAY	WEDNESDAY	THURSDAY
Breakfast				
Lunch				
Dinner				

	FRIDAY	SATURDAY	SUNDAY	NOTES
Breakfast				
Lunch				
Dinner				

Budget Planner

Expense	Amount	Due Date
UTILITIES		
Electric		
Gas		
Electric		
Electric		
Electric		
TRANSPORTATION		
Car Payment		
Gas		
Repair / Maintenance		
DEBT PAYMENTS		
Credit Card		
Others		
MISC.		
Groceries		
Personal Care		
Household items		
TOTAL		

	MONDAY	TUESDAY	WEDNESDAY	THURSDAY
Breakfast				
Lunch				
Dinner				

	FRIDAY	SATURDAY	SUNDAY	NOTES
Breakfast				
Lunch				
Dinner				

Budget Planner

Expense	Amount	Due Date
UTILITIES		
Electric		
Gas		
Electric		
Electric		
Electric		
TRANSPORTATION		
Car Payment		
Gas		
Repair / Maintenance		
DEBT PAYMENTS		
Credit Card		
Others		
MISC.		
Groceries		
Personal Care		
Household items		
TOTAL		

	MONDAY	TUESDAY	WEDNESDAY	THURSDAY
Breakfast				
Lunch				
Dinner				

	FRIDAY	SATURDAY	SUNDAY	NOTES
Breakfast				
Lunch				
Dinner				

Budget Planner

Expense	Amount	Due Date
UTILITIES		
Electric		
Gas		
Electric		
Electric		
Electric		
TRANSPORTATION		
Car Payment		
Gas		
Repair / Maintenance		
DEBT PAYMENTS		
Credit Card		
Others		
MISC.		
Groceries		
Personal Care		
Household items		
TOTAL		

	MONDAY	TUESDAY	WEDNESDAY	THURSDAY
Breakfast				
Lunch				
Dinner				

	FRIDAY	SATURDAY	SUNDAY	NOTES
Breakfast				
Lunch				
Dinner				

Budget Planner

Expense	Amount	Due Date
UTILITIES		
Electric		
Gas		
Electric		
Electric		
Electric		
TRANSPORTATION		
Car Payment		
Gas		
Repair / Maintenance		
DEBT PAYMENTS		
Credit Card		
Others		
MISC.		
Groceries		
Personal Care		
Household items		
TOTAL		

	MONDAY	TUESDAY	WEDNESDAY	THURSDAY
Breakfast				
Lunch				
Dinner				

	FRIDAY	SATURDAY	SUNDAY	NOTES
Breakfast				
Lunch				
Dinner				

Budget Planner

Expense	Amount	Due Date
UTILITIES		
Electric		
Gas		
Electric		
Electric		
Electric		
TRANSPORTATION		
Car Payment		
Gas		
Repair / Maintenance		
DEBT PAYMENTS		
Credit Card		
Others		
MISC.		
Groceries		
Personal Care		
Household items		
TOTAL		

	MONDAY	TUESDAY	WEDNESDAY	THURSDAY
Breakfast				
Lunch				
Dinner				

	FRIDAY	SATURDAY	SUNDAY	NOTES
Breakfast				
Lunch				
Dinner				

Budget Planner

Expense	Amount	Due Date
UTILITIES		
Electric		
Gas		
Electric		
Electric		
Electric		
TRANSPORTATION		
Car Payment		
Gas		
Repair / Maintenance		
DEBT PAYMENTS		
Credit Card		
Others		
MISC.		
Groceries		
Personal Care		
Household items		
TOTAL		

	MONDAY	TUESDAY	WEDNESDAY	THURSDAY
Breakfast				
Lunch				
Dinner				

	FRIDAY	SATURDAY	SUNDAY	NOTES
Breakfast				
Lunch				
Dinner				

Budget Planner

Expense	Amount	Due Date
UTILITIES		
Electric		
Gas		
Electric		
Electric		
Electric		
TRANSPORTATION		
Car Payment		
Gas		
Repair / Maintenance		
DEBT PAYMENTS		
Credit Card		
Others		
MISC.		
Groceries		
Personal Care		
Household items		
TOTAL		

	MONDAY	TUESDAY	WEDNESDAY	THURSDAY
Breakfast				
Lunch				
Dinner				

	FRIDAY	SATURDAY	SUNDAY	NOTES
Breakfast				
Lunch				
Dinner				

Budget Planner

Expense	Amount	Due Date
UTILITIES		
Electric		
Gas		
Electric		
Electric		
Electric		
TRANSPORTATION		
Car Payment		
Gas		
Repair / Maintenance		
DEBT PAYMENTS		
Credit Card		
Others		
MISC.		
Groceries		
Personal Care		
Household items		
TOTAL		

	MONDAY	TUESDAY	WEDNESDAY	THURSDAY
Breakfast				
Lunch				
Dinner				

	FRIDAY	SATURDAY	SUNDAY	NOTES
Breakfast				
Lunch				
Dinner				

Budget Planner

Expense	Amount	Due Date
UTILITIES		
Electric		
Gas		
Electric		
Electric		
Electric		
TRANSPORTATION		
Car Payment		
Gas		
Repair / Maintenance		
DEBT PAYMENTS		
Credit Card		
Others		
MISC.		
Groceries		
Personal Care		
Household items		
TOTAL		

	MONDAY	TUESDAY	WEDNESDAY	THURSDAY
Breakfast				
Lunch				
Dinner				

	FRIDAY	SATURDAY	SUNDAY	NOTES
Breakfast				
Lunch				
Dinner				

Budget Planner

Expense	Amount	Due Date
UTILITIES		
Electric		
Gas		
Electric		
Electric		
Electric		
TRANSPORTATION		
Car Payment		
Gas		
Repair / Maintenance		
DEBT PAYMENTS		
Credit Card		
Others		
MISC.		
Groceries		
Personal Care		
Household items		
TOTAL		

	MONDAY	TUESDAY	WEDNESDAY	THURSDAY
Breakfast				
Lunch				
Dinner				

	FRIDAY	SATURDAY	SUNDAY	NOTES
Breakfast				
Lunch				
Dinner				

Budget Planner

Expense	Amount	Due Date
UTILITIES		
Electric		
Gas		
Electric		
Electric		
Electric		
TRANSPORTATION		
Car Payment		
Gas		
Repair / Maintenance		
DEBT PAYMENTS		
Credit Card		
Others		
MISC.		
Groceries		
Personal Care		
Household items		
TOTAL		

	MONDAY	TUESDAY	WEDNESDAY	THURSDAY
Breakfast				
Lunch				
Dinner				

	FRIDAY	SATURDAY	SUNDAY	NOTES
Breakfast				
Lunch				
Dinner				

Budget Planner

Expense	Amount	Due Date
UTILITIES		
Electric		
Gas		
Electric		
Electric		
Electric		
TRANSPORTATION		
Car Payment		
Gas		
Repair / Maintenance		
DEBT PAYMENTS		
Credit Card		
Others		
MISC.		
Groceries		
Personal Care		
Household items		
TOTAL		

	MONDAY	TUESDAY	WEDNESDAY	THURSDAY
Breakfast				
Lunch				
Dinner				

	FRIDAY	SATURDAY	SUNDAY	NOTES
Breakfast				
Lunch				
Dinner				

Budget Planner

Expense	Amount	Due Date
UTILITIES		
Electric		
Gas		
Electric		
Electric		
Electric		
TRANSPORTATION		
Car Payment		
Gas		
Repair / Maintenance		
DEBT PAYMENTS		
Credit Card		
Others		
MISC.		
Groceries		
Personal Care		
Household items		
TOTAL		

	MONDAY	TUESDAY	WEDNESDAY	THURSDAY
Breakfast				
Lunch				
Dinner				

	FRIDAY	SATURDAY	SUNDAY	NOTES
Breakfast				
Lunch				
Dinner				

Budget Planner

Expense	Amount	Due Date
UTILITIES		
Electric		
Gas		
Electric		
Electric		
Electric		
TRANSPORTATION		
Car Payment		
Gas		
Repair / Maintenance		
DEBT PAYMENTS		
Credit Card		
Others		
MISC.		
Groceries		
Personal Care		
Household items		
TOTAL		

	MONDAY	TUESDAY	WEDNESDAY	THURSDAY
Breakfast				
Lunch				
Dinner				

	FRIDAY	SATURDAY	SUNDAY	NOTES
Breakfast				
Lunch				
Dinner				

Budget Planner

Expense	Amount	Due Date
UTILITIES		
Electric		
Gas		
Electric		
Electric		
Electric		
TRANSPORTATION		
Car Payment		
Gas		
Repair / Maintenance		
DEBT PAYMENTS		
Credit Card		
Others		
MISC.		
Groceries		
Personal Care		
Household items		
TOTAL		

	MONDAY	TUESDAY	WEDNESDAY	THURSDAY
Breakfast				
Lunch				
Dinner				

	FRIDAY	SATURDAY	SUNDAY	NOTES
Breakfast				
Lunch				
Dinner				

Budget Planner

Expense	Amount	Due Date
UTILITIES		
Electric		
Gas		
Electric		
Electric		
Electric		
TRANSPORTATION		
Car Payment		
Gas		
Repair / Maintenance		
DEBT PAYMENTS		
Credit Card		
Others		
MISC.		
Groceries		
Personal Care		
Household items		
TOTAL		

	MONDAY	TUESDAY	WEDNESDAY	THURSDAY
Breakfast				
Lunch				
Dinner				

	FRIDAY	SATURDAY	SUNDAY	NOTES
Breakfast				
Lunch				
Dinner				

Budget Planner

Expense	Amount	Due Date
UTILITIES		
Electric		
Gas		
Electric		
Electric		
Electric		
TRANSPORTATION		
Car Payment		
Gas		
Repair / Maintenance		
DEBT PAYMENTS		
Credit Card		
Others		
MISC.		
Groceries		
Personal Care		
Household items		
TOTAL		

	MONDAY	TUESDAY	WEDNESDAY	THURSDAY
Breakfast				
Lunch				
Dinner				

	FRIDAY	SATURDAY	SUNDAY	NOTES
Breakfast				
Lunch				
Dinner				

Budget Planner

Expense	Amount	Due Date
UTILITIES		
Electric		
Gas		
Electric		
Electric		
Electric		
TRANSPORTATION		
Car Payment		
Gas		
Repair / Maintenance		
DEBT PAYMENTS		
Credit Card		
Others		
MISC.		
Groceries		
Personal Care		
Household items		
TOTAL		

	MONDAY	TUESDAY	WEDNESDAY	THURSDAY
Breakfast				
Lunch				
Dinner				

	FRIDAY	SATURDAY	SUNDAY	NOTES
Breakfast				
Lunch				
Dinner				

Budget Planner

Expense	Amount	Due Date
UTILITIES		
Electric		
Gas		
Electric		
Electric		
Electric		
TRANSPORTATION		
Car Payment		
Gas		
Repair / Maintenance		
DEBT PAYMENTS		
Credit Card		
Others		
MISC.		
Groceries		
Personal Care		
Household items		
TOTAL		

	MONDAY	TUESDAY	WEDNESDAY	THURSDAY
Breakfast				
Lunch				
Dinner				

	FRIDAY	SATURDAY	SUNDAY	NOTES
Breakfast				
Lunch				
Dinner				

Budget Planner

Expense	Amount	Due Date
UTILITIES		
Electric		
Gas		
Electric		
Electric		
Electric		
TRANSPORTATION		
Car Payment		
Gas		
Repair / Maintenance		
DEBT PAYMENTS		
Credit Card		
Others		
MISC.		
Groceries		
Personal Care		
Household items		
TOTAL		

	MONDAY	TUESDAY	WEDNESDAY	THURSDAY
Breakfast				
Lunch				
Dinner				

	FRIDAY	SATURDAY	SUNDAY	NOTES
Breakfast				
Lunch				
Dinner				

Budget Planner

Expense	Amount	Due Date
UTILITIES		
Electric		
Gas		
Electric		
Electric		
Electric		
TRANSPORTATION		
Car Payment		
Gas		
Repair / Maintenance		
DEBT PAYMENTS		
Credit Card		
Others		
MISC.		
Groceries		
Personal Care		
Household items		
TOTAL		

	MONDAY	TUESDAY	WEDNESDAY	THURSDAY
Breakfast				
Lunch				
Dinner				

	FRIDAY	SATURDAY	SUNDAY	NOTES
Breakfast				
Lunch				
Dinner				

Budget Planner

Expense	Amount	Due Date
UTILITIES		
Electric		
Gas		
Electric		
Electric		
Electric		
TRANSPORTATION		
Car Payment		
Gas		
Repair / Maintenance		
DEBT PAYMENTS		
Credit Card		
Others		
MISC.		
Groceries		
Personal Care		
Household items		
TOTAL		

	MONDAY	TUESDAY	WEDNESDAY	THURSDAY
Breakfast				
Lunch				
Dinner				

	FRIDAY	SATURDAY	SUNDAY	NOTES
Breakfast				
Lunch				
Dinner				

Budget Planner

Expense	Amount	Due Date
UTILITIES		
Electric		
Gas		
Electric		
Electric		
Electric		
TRANSPORTATION		
Car Payment		
Gas		
Repair / Maintenance		
DEBT PAYMENTS		
Credit Card		
Others		
MISC.		
Groceries		
Personal Care		
Household items		
TOTAL		

	MONDAY	TUESDAY	WEDNESDAY	THURSDAY
Breakfast				
Lunch				
Dinner				

	FRIDAY	SATURDAY	SUNDAY	NOTES
Breakfast				
Lunch				
Dinner				

Budget Planner

Expense	Amount	Due Date
UTILITIES		
Electric		
Gas		
Electric		
Electric		
Electric		
TRANSPORTATION		
Car Payment		
Gas		
Repair / Maintenance		
DEBT PAYMENTS		
Credit Card		
Others		
MISC.		
Groceries		
Personal Care		
Household items		
TOTAL		

	MONDAY	TUESDAY	WEDNESDAY	THURSDAY
Breakfast				
Lunch				
Dinner				

	FRIDAY	SATURDAY	SUNDAY	NOTES
Breakfast				
Lunch				
Dinner				

Budget Planner

Expense	Amount	Due Date
UTILITIES		
Electric		
Gas		
Electric		
Electric		
Electric		
TRANSPORTATION		
Car Payment		
Gas		
Repair / Maintenance		
DEBT PAYMENTS		
Credit Card		
Others		
MISC.		
Groceries		
Personal Care		
Household items		
TOTAL		

	MONDAY	TUESDAY	WEDNESDAY	THURSDAY
Breakfast				
Lunch				
Dinner				

	FRIDAY	SATURDAY	SUNDAY	NOTES
Breakfast				
Lunch				
Dinner				

Budget Planner

Expense	Amount	Due Date
UTILITIES		
Electric		
Gas		
Electric		
Electric		
Electric		
TRANSPORTATION		
Car Payment		
Gas		
Repair / Maintenance		
DEBT PAYMENTS		
Credit Card		
Others		
MISC.		
Groceries		
Personal Care		
Household items		
TOTAL		

	MONDAY	TUESDAY	WEDNESDAY	THURSDAY
Breakfast				
Lunch				
Dinner				

	FRIDAY	SATURDAY	SUNDAY	NOTES
Breakfast				
Lunch				
Dinner				

Budget Planner

Expense	Amount	Due Date
UTILITIES		
Electric		
Gas		
Electric		
Electric		
Electric		
TRANSPORTATION		
Car Payment		
Gas		
Repair / Maintenance		
DEBT PAYMENTS		
Credit Card		
Others		
MISC.		
Groceries		
Personal Care		
Household items		
TOTAL		

	MONDAY	TUESDAY	WEDNESDAY	THURSDAY
Breakfast				
Lunch				
Dinner				

	FRIDAY	SATURDAY	SUNDAY	NOTES
Breakfast				
Lunch				
Dinner				

Budget Planner

Expense	Amount	Due Date
UTILITIES		
Electric		
Gas		
Electric		
Electric		
Electric		
TRANSPORTATION		
Car Payment		
Gas		
Repair / Maintenance		
DEBT PAYMENTS		
Credit Card		
Others		
MISC.		
Groceries		
Personal Care		
Household items		
TOTAL		

	MONDAY	TUESDAY	WEDNESDAY	THURSDAY
Breakfast				
Lunch				
Dinner				

	FRIDAY	SATURDAY	SUNDAY	NOTES
Breakfast				
Lunch				
Dinner				

Budget Planner

Expense	Amount	Due Date
UTILITIES		
Electric		
Gas		
Electric		
Electric		
Electric		
TRANSPORTATION		
Car Payment		
Gas		
Repair / Maintenance		
DEBT PAYMENTS		
Credit Card		
Others		
MISC.		
Groceries		
Personal Care		
Household items		
TOTAL		

	MONDAY	TUESDAY	WEDNESDAY	THURSDAY
Breakfast				
Lunch				
Dinner				

	FRIDAY	SATURDAY	SUNDAY	NOTES
Breakfast				
Lunch				
Dinner				

Budget Planner

Expense	Amount	Due Date
UTILITIES		
Electric		
Gas		
Electric		
Electric		
Electric		
TRANSPORTATION		
Car Payment		
Gas		
Repair / Maintenance		
DEBT PAYMENTS		
Credit Card		
Others		
MISC.		
Groceries		
Personal Care		
Household items		
TOTAL		

	MONDAY	TUESDAY	WEDNESDAY	THURSDAY
Breakfast				
Lunch				
Dinner				

	FRIDAY	SATURDAY	SUNDAY	NOTES
Breakfast				
Lunch				
Dinner				

Budget Planner

Expense	Amount	Due Date
UTILITIES		
Electric		
Gas		
Electric		
Electric		
Electric		
TRANSPORTATION		
Car Payment		
Gas		
Repair / Maintenance		
DEBT PAYMENTS		
Credit Card		
Others		
MISC.		
Groceries		
Personal Care		
Household items		
TOTAL		

	MONDAY	TUESDAY	WEDNESDAY	THURSDAY
Breakfast				
Lunch				
Dinner				

	FRIDAY	SATURDAY	SUNDAY	NOTES
Breakfast				
Lunch				
Dinner				

Budget Planner

Expense	Amount	Due Date
UTILITIES		
Electric		
Gas		
Electric		
Electric		
Electric		
TRANSPORTATION		
Car Payment		
Gas		
Repair / Maintenance		
DEBT PAYMENTS		
Credit Card		
Others		
MISC.		
Groceries		
Personal Care		
Household items		
TOTAL		

	MONDAY	TUESDAY	WEDNESDAY	THURSDAY
Breakfast				
Lunch				
Dinner				

	FRIDAY	SATURDAY	SUNDAY	NOTES
Breakfast				
Lunch				
Dinner				

Budget Planner

Expense	Amount	Due Date
UTILITIES		
Electric		
Gas		
Electric		
Electric		
Electric		
TRANSPORTATION		
Car Payment		
Gas		
Repair / Maintenance		
DEBT PAYMENTS		
Credit Card		
Others		
MISC.		
Groceries		
Personal Care		
Household items		
TOTAL		

	MONDAY	TUESDAY	WEDNESDAY	THURSDAY
Breakfast				
Lunch				
Dinner				

	FRIDAY	SATURDAY	SUNDAY	NOTES
Breakfast				
Lunch				
Dinner				

Budget Planner

Expense	Amount	Due Date
UTILITIES		
Electric		
Gas		
Electric		
Electric		
Electric		
TRANSPORTATION		
Car Payment		
Gas		
Repair / Maintenance		
DEBT PAYMENTS		
Credit Card		
Others		
MISC.		
Groceries		
Personal Care		
Household items		
TOTAL		

	MONDAY	TUESDAY	WEDNESDAY	THURSDAY
Breakfast				
Lunch				
Dinner				

	FRIDAY	SATURDAY	SUNDAY	NOTES
Breakfast				
Lunch				
Dinner				

Budget Planner

Expense	Amount	Due Date
UTILITIES		
Electric		
Gas		
Electric		
Electric		
Electric		
TRANSPORTATION		
Car Payment		
Gas		
Repair / Maintenance		
DEBT PAYMENTS		
Credit Card		
Others		
MISC.		
Groceries		
Personal Care		
Household items		
TOTAL		

	MONDAY	TUESDAY	WEDNESDAY	THURSDAY
Breakfast				
Lunch				
Dinner				

	FRIDAY	SATURDAY	SUNDAY	NOTES
Breakfast				
Lunch				
Dinner				

Budget Planner

Expense	Amount	Due Date
UTILITIES		
Electric		
Gas		
Electric		
Electric		
Electric		
TRANSPORTATION		
Car Payment		
Gas		
Repair / Maintenance		
DEBT PAYMENTS		
Credit Card		
Others		
MISC.		
Groceries		
Personal Care		
Household items		
TOTAL		

	MONDAY	TUESDAY	WEDNESDAY	THURSDAY
Breakfast				
Lunch				
Dinner				

	FRIDAY	SATURDAY	SUNDAY	NOTES
Breakfast				
Lunch				
Dinner				

Budget Planner

Expense	Amount	Due Date
UTILITIES		
Electric		
Gas		
Electric		
Electric		
Electric		
TRANSPORTATION		
Car Payment		
Gas		
Repair / Maintenance		
DEBT PAYMENTS		
Credit Card		
Others		
MISC.		
Groceries		
Personal Care		
Household items		
TOTAL		

	MONDAY	TUESDAY	WEDNESDAY	THURSDAY
Breakfast				
Lunch				
Dinner				

	FRIDAY	SATURDAY	SUNDAY	NOTES
Breakfast				
Lunch				
Dinner				

Budget Planner

Expense	Amount	Due Date
UTILITIES		
Electric		
Gas		
Electric		
Electric		
Electric		
TRANSPORTATION		
Car Payment		
Gas		
Repair / Maintenance		
DEBT PAYMENTS		
Credit Card		
Others		
MISC.		
Groceries		
Personal Care		
Household items		
TOTAL		

www.ingramcontent.com/pod-product-compliance
Lightning Source LLC
Chambersburg PA
CBHW081438220526
45466CB00008B/2432